The Essential
CHINESE
COOKBOOK

The Essential
CHINESE
COOKBOOK

50 CLASSIC RECIPES,
WITH STEP-BY-STEP PHOTOGRAPHS

EDITED BY
HEATHER THOMAS

COURAGE
BOOKS
AN IMPRINT OF RUNNING PRESS
PHILADELPHIA • LONDON

Printed in Hong Kong

9 8 7 6 5 4 3 2 1

Digit on the right indicates the number of this printing

Library of Congress Cataloging-in-Publication Number
97-66809

ISBN 0-7624-0278-4

Designed and produced by SP Creative Design
Wickham Skeith, Suffolk, England
Editor and writer: Heather Thomas
Art director: Al Rockall
Designer: Rolando Ugolini
Special photography: Phil Webb
Step-by-step photography: GGS Photographics, Norwich
Food preparation: Jo Craig, Dawn Stock and Caroline Stevens
Styling: Helen Payne
Produced by Mandarin Offset

Published by Courage Books, an imprint of
Running Press Book Publishers
125 South Twenty-second Street
Philadelphia, Pennsylvania 19103-4399

Notes

1. Standard spoon measurements are used in all recipes.

2. Eggs should be large unless otherwise stated.

3. Whole milk should be used unless otherwise stated.

4. Fresh herbs should be used unless otherwise stated.
If unavailable, use dried herbs as an alternative, but halve
the quantities stated.

5. Ovens should be preheated to the specified temperature. If
using a convection oven, follow the manufacturer's instructions for
adjusting the time and the temperature.

CONTENTS

INTRODUCTION

China is such a vast country that the styles of cuisine and regional dishes are extremely varied and reflect both the changes in climate and geography, and the foods grown. There are four main regional cookery schools. The Eastern School, which includes the fertile Yangtse Basin, Shanghai, and the provinces of Jiangsi and Fujian, has many speciality fish and rice dishes. The Southern School is regarded as the jewel of Chinese cuisine and includes Canton and the province of Guangdong. The Western School specializes in spicy, piquant food from Szechuan province, whereas the Northern School is the oldest of the four and encompasses the cuisines of Beijing, Shandong, and Henan.

Chinese food is incredibly diverse and can be refined and delicate, or robust and earthy. However, what is common to all Chinese dishes is the necessity of using only the freshest ingredients. Vegetables are often gathered immediately before cooking, and poultry and fish are often bought alive. To the Chinese, loss of freshness means loss of flavor.

A Chinese meal consists of many dishes, all carefully selected so as to complement and balance each other in texture, flavor, shape, and color. It is a very healthy cuisine: many dishes are steamed or quickly stir-fried in the minimum of oil (*ch'ao*). The ingredients to be stir-fried are usually cut into strips or dice so that they cook through quickly and the maximum food surface is in contact with the heat. They are cooked in a wok, a traditional Chinese round-bottomed pan, and are kept in continuous motion as the cook moves and tosses them in the hot oil or sauce. The short cooking time, literally in minutes, helps to preserve the nutrients and natural flavors of the food and means that it is eaten really fresh.

The most time-consuming part of creating a Chinese meal, with its range of different dishes, is in its preparation. Many of the ingredients are cut into chunks, shreds, strips, dice, or cubes, and elaborate garnishes are sometimes prepared. However, you can do all this in advance earlier in the day and store in the refrigerator until it is time to cook the meal.

Bamboo shoots

These are the tender, edible shoots of certain bamboo plants which are harvested at the end of the rainy season. In China, they may be used fresh or canned. They have a distinctive crunchy texture and are often sliced and added to stir-fried dishes. They are available in cans in Western countries and can be stored in fresh water in the refrigerator for up to seven days after opening.

Bean curd

This is also known as doufu or tofu, and is sold in white blocks. It is extremely healthy and nutritious, being rich in protein and low in fat. Made from puréed yellow soy beans, it has a bland flavor and is often used in soups and stir-fries. Fresh bean curd can be covered and kept in the refrigerator for several days.

Bean sprouts

These are the crisp, crunchy sprouts of mung or soy beans. They are an essential

ingredient in many stir-fried and savory dishes. They can be kept in the salad crisper compartment of a refrigerator.

Black beans

These small fermented black soy beans have a salty flavor and are often ground into a paste and mixed with spices before being bottled as black bean sauce.

Chiles

Both fresh and dried chiles are used in Chinese cooking. Fiery fresh red ones are widely used in the western and northern regions, whereas dried chiles are common in spicy Szechuan dishes. Chiles are used to flavor cooking oils, are ground into powder, and may be made into a variety of hot, spicy sauces. Chilli dipping sauce is fiery and a brilliant red, and is usually made from a mixture of chiles, vinegar, salt, and sugar.

Always take care when handling fresh chiles. Wear protective gloves or wash your hands thoroughly afterward. Avoid contact with your eyes and delicate skin as the seeds can burn you.

Chinese mushrooms

These fragrant dried mushrooms have a distinctive smoky flavor and are sold in many delicatessens and Chinese speciality stores. They must be soaked and reconstituted in warm water before cooking; the stems are discarded.

Cilantro

Together with chives, this is the herb that is most commonly used in Chinese cookery. Sometimes referred to as Chinese parsley, it is used to flavor and garnish many fish and chicken dishes.

Cornstarch

This is widely used as a thickening agent in sauces and batters, and in marinades to coat such foods as chicken, pork, and shrimp. It is always blended with cold water, Chinese wine, or other liquids before being added to a sauce.

Five-spice powder

This is a fragrant mixture of ground star anise, spicy Szechuan peppercorns, fennel, cloves, and cinnamon. It is used to flavor many Chinese savory dishes, especially red-cooked meat and poultry.

Flour

In China, flour may be made with wheat, ground raw rice, or pearl rice. Rice flour is often used to make the dough for dim sum (snack) dumplings.

Gingerroot

Sometimes called green ginger, fresh gingerroot is used widely to flavor soups, meat, fish, and vegetable dishes. It must be peeled before using and is then sliced, chopped or crushed. If you wish to keep ginger fresh for several months, you can peel it and preserve it in a screwtop jar filled with sherry or rice wine. The ginger can then be used as required, and the

sherry will be infused with a marvellous ginger flavor and can be added to many dishes. The Chinese have a sweet tooth and also use candied stem ginger in many desserts.

Hoisin sauce

This thick dark brown sauce is made from soy beans, sugar, flour, garlic, chiles, vinegar, salt, and sesame seed oil. It is sold in jars and is available in most markets. It is often used to marinade meat, and is sometimes known as barbecue sauce.

Lychees

These delicately flavored fruit are beloved of the Chinese and appear in our shops at Christmastime. The fragrant white flesh is enclosed in a hard pink shell, which can be peeled away. They can be bought in cans all the year round.

Noodles

These are eaten at nearly all Chinese meals and may be made from wheat, sometimes enriched with egg, or rice, or ground mung beans (transparent or cellophane noodles). They may be purchased dried or fresh, and there are many varieties.

Rice noodles should be soaked in warm water until they are soft and then they may be stir-fried with vegetables or added to soups and other cooked dishes. Transparent noodles are available dried and are soaked before using. They are often deep-fried.

Oils

These may be made either from corn, sunflowers, rapeseed, soybeans, cottonseed, peanuts, or sesame seeds. They are used in stir-frying and deep-frying as well as to flavor food. The most distinctive and strongly flavored is sesame oil, which is often used in marinades or may be sprinkled on savory dishes immediately before serving. Oils are often flavored with aromatics and fiery chiles.

Oyster sauce

This is a common ingredient in Cantonese cooking. Although it is made from oysters and soy sauce, surprizingly it does not have a fishy flavor.

Rice

Who could imagine a Chinese meal without rice? Long-grain, short-grain, and pearl varieties are all used. Pearl rice has a sticky texture and is often cooked wrapped in lotus leaves. In China, rice is always washed several times in clean water before cooking.

Rice wine

This is used in cooking, especially in marinades and sauces, as well as for drinking. If you cannot obtain it, a dry sherry will make an adequate substitute.

Sesame seeds

Dried sesame seeds are used for flavoring many dishes. Sometimes the seeds are lightly toasted or roasted before using. They may also be used for making sesame oil, or ground into paste.

Soy sauce

This is an essential ingredient in Chinese cookery. It is made from fermented soy beans and may be light or dark in color. Light soy sauce has a salty flavor and is considered superior to dark soy sauce.

Star anise

This amazing star-shaped seed pod from the anise plant has an unusual liquorice flavor and is used in five-spice powder.

Water chestnuts

These are not really chestnuts at all, but walnut-sized bulbs. The crisp white flesh is enclosed in a brown skin and has a sweet flavor. In America, they may be bought in cans and are usually rinsed and sliced before adding to savory dishes.

Won ton skins

Although you can make these yourself, it is easier to buy them ready-made. They are available fresh or frozen in Chinese supermarkets and many delicatessens. Made from wheat flour, egg and water, they are filled with minced savory mixtures of fish, meat, or vegetables, and are then boiled, steamed, or fried.

Yellow bean sauce

This thick spicy sauce is sold in jars in most supermarkets, and is made from fermented yellow beans.

Utensils and equipment

In the Chinese kitchen, there are certain essential cooking utensils. If you wish to cook authentic Chinese food yourself at home, it is worth investing in these. They can be purchased in Chinese supermarkets and kitchen shops.

Cleavers: Chinese cooks use these for everything; they are particularly useful for chopping up chicken and ducks.

Steamers: Usually made from bamboo, these come in an assortment of different sizes. The food to be steamed is placed inside and the steamer is then put over a wok or pot of boiling or simmering water. If you are steaming more than one dish, the steamers can often be stacked on top of each other.

Woks: These iron or steel pans have a rounded base to improve heat distribution. The shape means that the heat is spread more evenly over the surface, making it ideal for rapid stir-frying. Woks can be bought in different sizes and are also useful for deep-frying.

SWEETCORN AND CRAB SOUP

Xiaren tang

1 Put the chopped gingerroot in a bowl and add the crabmeat and sherry. Mix well together and then set aside.

2 In a separate bowl, beat the egg white, and set aside. Mix the cornstarch with the water to make a smooth paste.

3 Put the broth in a large saucepan and bring to a rolling boil. Add the salt, corn kernels, and the crabmeat and ginger mixture.

4 Bring the broth back to the boil, and then add the cornstarch paste, stirring constantly. When the soup thickens, stir in the egg white and then serve very hot, garnished with shredded scallions.

PREPARATION: 10 MINUTES
COOKING: 8 TO 10 MINUTES
SERVES: 4

1 teaspoon finely chopped fresh gingerroot
1/2 cup crabmeat
2 teaspoons dry sherry
1 egg white
3 teaspoons cornstarch
2 tablespoons cold water
2 1/2 cups clear broth (see page 110)
1 teaspoon salt
1 cup corn kernels
To garnish:
1 scallion, finely chopped

BEAN CURD AND SHRIMP SOUP

Doufou xiaren tang

1 Put the peeled shrimp in a small bowl. In another bowl, break up the egg white with a fork and then add to the shrimp and mix well.

2 Cut the ham into small dice, approximately the same size as the peas. Next cut the bean curd into cubes of a similar size.

½ cup cooked peeled shrimp
1 egg white
2 ounces cooked ham
4 ounces bean curd
2½ cups clear broth (see page 110)
¼ cup peas, fresh or frozen
1 tablespoon soy sauce
1 tablespoon cornstarch
salt and freshly ground black pepper

PREPARATION: 10 MINUTES
COOKING: 10 TO 15 MINUTES
SERVES: 4

3 Put the clear broth in a saucepan and bring to the boil. Add the ham, bean curd, and peas, and when it starts to bubble again, add the soy sauce and shrimp. Boil hard for 20 seconds.

4 Mix the cornstarch with a little cold water and then pour it into the soup, stirring constantly. When it thickens, season to taste with salt and pepper. Serve immediately.

HOT AND SOUR SOUP

Suan ha tang

4 Chinese dried mushrooms
4 ounces boneless cooked chicken meat, skinned
4 ounces firm bean curd
3 ounces bamboo shoots
1 egg
salt
2 ½ cups clear broth (see page 110)
½ cup peas, fresh or frozen
2 tablespoons vinegar
1 tablespoon dark soy sauce
2 teaspoons freshly ground black pepper
3 tablespoons cornstarch

1 Put the mushrooms in a bowl, cover with warm water and leave to soak for 20 to 25 minutes. Drain and reserve the soaking liquid. Squeeze the mushrooms dry and cut into thin shreds. Discard the hard stalks.

3 Pour the broth into a saucepan with the reserved soaking liquid from the mushrooms. Bring to the boil. Add the mushrooms, chicken, bean curd, bamboo shoots, peas, and 1 teaspoon of salt. Cook for 2 minutes and add the vinegar, soy sauce, and pepper.

2 Thinly shred the chicken, bean curd and bamboo shoots. Break the egg into a bowl, add a pinch of salt and beat lightly together.

4 Mix the cornstarch to a smooth paste with 6 tablespoons of cold water. Add to the soup, stirring until it thickens. Add the beaten egg very slowly in a thin, steady stream, pouring it evenly all over the surface of the soup. Serve hot.

PREPARATION:
15 MINUTES + SOAKING TIME
COOKING: 15 MINUTES
SERVES: 4

WON TON SOUP

Wahn tan tang

1 To make the filling for the won tons, put the ground pork in a bowl and add the spinach leaves, salt, sugar, and sherry. Mix well together.

2 Put the won ton skins on a lightly floured surface and place one teaspoonful of the pork and spinach filling in the center of each skin.

3 Bring the opposite corners of each won ton skin together in a fold and pinch the top edges together firmly to seal. Fold the other two corners towards each other and seal.

3/4 cup ground pork
4 ounces spinach leaves, chopped
1/2 teaspoon salt
1 teaspoon sugar
1 tablespoon sherry
24 won ton skins
3³/4 cups clear broth (see page 110)
To garnish:
1 scallion, finely chopped

PREPARATION: 20 MINUTES
COOKING: 7 TO 8 MINUTES
SERVES: 4 TO 6

4 Put the broth in a large saucepan and bring to the boil. Drop in the filled won tons and boil rapidly for 2 to 3 minutes. Serve immediately, garnished with chopped scallion.

CRISPY SEAWEED

Cai soong

1 Separate the leaves of the summer cabbage. Wash them well in a colander and then pat dry with paper towels.

2 Using a very sharp knife, shred the cabbage into the thinnest possible shavings. Spread the shavings out on paper towels for about 30 minutes, until thoroughly dry.

| 1½ pounds summer cabbage |
| vegetable oil for deep-frying |
| 1½ teaspoons sugar |
| 1 teaspoon salt |

3 Heat the oil in a wok or a deep-fat fryer. Turn off the heat for 30 seconds and then add a small batch of cabbage shavings. Turn up the heat to moderate and deep-fry the cabbage until the shavings begin to float on the surface of the oil. Take care as they tend to spit while they are cooking.

4 Remove from the wok with a perforated spoon and drain on paper towels. Cook the remaining cabbage in batches in the same way. When it is all cooked, transfer to a bowl and sprinkle over the sugar and salt. Toss gently to mix and serve either warm or cold as an appetizer.

PREPARATION: 10 MINUTES +
DRYING TIME
COOKING: 10 MINUTES
SERVES: 8

FIVE-SPICE PORK RIBS

Wuxiang paigu

2 pounds pork ribs
For the marinade:
1 teaspoon salt
2 tablespoons sugar
2 tablespoons brandy or vodka
2 tablespoons light soy sauce
2 tablespoons hoisin sauce
1 tablespoon dark soy sauce
1 teaspoon five-spice powder
1 teaspoon curry powder (optional)

2 During this time, turn the ribs over once or twice so that they are well covered with the marinade and really absorb the flavors.

1 Cut the pork into individual ribs if this has not been done already. Place them in a large ovenproof dish. Mix all the marinade ingredients together and pour over the pork ribs. Leave in a cool place or the refrigerator to marinate for 1 hour.

PREPARATION: 5 MINUTES +
MARINATING TIME
COOKING: 40 TO 45 MINUTES
SERVES: 4 TO 6

3 Place the dish in a preheated oven at 400°F and cook for 40 to 45 minutes, turning them once, halfway through cooking. Alternatively, you can remove the ribs from the marinade and cook under a hot broiler or on a grill for 15 to 20 minutes, turning them occasionally and brushing with marinade, until evenly browned.

4 Chop each rib into 2 or 3 bite-sized pieces with a meat cleaver, if you have one, or serve whole with the sauce poured over them. If you have grilled or broiled the ribs, boil up the marinade in a saucepan with a little meat broth or water to make the sauce.

DEEP-FRIED WON TONS

Cha wahn tan

24 won ton skins
vegetable oil for deep-frying
For the filling:
1/2 cup ground pork
1/2 cup cooked peeled shrimp, finely chopped
2 teaspoons finely chopped scallion
1 tablespoon Chinese rice wine or dry sherry
1 teaspoon sugar
1/2 teaspoon salt
For the sauce:
1 tablespoon cornstarch
1 tablespoon tomato paste
1 tablespoon sugar
2 tablespoons vinegar
1 tablespoon soy sauce
1 tablespoon vegetable oil

1 Make the filling: put all the filling ingredients in a small bowl and mix thoroughly together to form a smooth mixture.

2 On a lightly floured surface, put 1 teaspoonful of the filling on each won ton skin. Fold over from corner to corner, wetting a small part of the skin on the sides immediately around the filling. Press them together firmly.

3 Heat the oil in a deep wok or deep-fat fryer until it is very hot. Turn the heat down and then fry the won tons in batches, for 2 to 3 minutes, or until crispy. Remove and drain on paper towels. Keep warm in a low oven.

4 Make the sauce: put the cornstarch in a bowl and mix to a paste with 4 to 5 tablespoons of cold water. Stir in the remaining ingredients, except the oil. Heat the oil in a wok or small saucepan and pour in the sauce mixture. Stir over moderate heat for 3 to 4 minutes until smooth. Serve immediately with the won tons.

PREPARATION: 30 MINUTES
COOKING: 10 MINUTES
SERVES: 4 TO 6

CRAB ROLLS

Xierou jiao

1 Make the wrapping: sift the flour and salt into a bowl and gradually beat in the water and eggs to form a smooth batter. Place a small, lightly oiled skillet over moderate heat and pour in 4 tablespoons of batter, rotating it until the base is covered. Cook until the edges curl, then flip over and cook the other side. Cook all the crepes in this way.

3 Place 2 tablespoons of the filling on half of each wrapping crepe. Fold the other half over and then fold the right side in toward the left, and the left side in toward the right. Roll up tightly and seal with the flour paste.

vegetable oil for deep-frying
For the wrapping:
4 tablespoons flour
¹⁄₂ teaspoon salt
4 tablespoons water
4 eggs, beaten
For the filling:
2 tablespoons oil
1 egg, beaten
1 scallion, shredded
1¹⁄₂ cups crabmeat, flaked
1 tablespoon dry sherry
salt and freshly ground black pepper
1 tablespoon cornstarch
For the flour paste:
1 tablespoon flour, mixed with 1 tablespoon water

2 Make the filling: heat the oil in a wok and add the egg, scallion, and crabmeat. Stir-fry for a few seconds and then add the sherry, salt, and pepper. Dissolve the cornstarch in 3 tablespoons of water and add to the wok, stirring until thickened. Remove from the heat and cool.

4 Heat the oil to 350°F, or until a cube of bread browns in 30 seconds, and deep-fry the crab rolls, a few at a time, until golden brown all over. Drain on paper towels and then cut into pieces diagonally. Serve the crab rolls immediately.

PREPARATION: 30 MINUTES
COOKING: 10 MINUTES
SERVES: 6 TO 8

STEAMED CHICKEN DUMPLINGS
Baozi

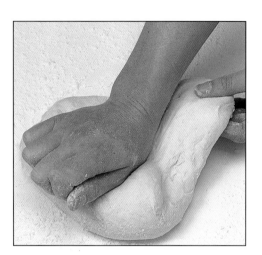

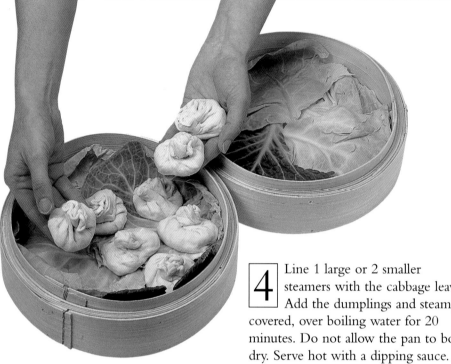

1 Sift the flour into a large mixing bowl and pour in the water. Mix thoroughly to form a stiff dough. Knead for 5 minutes and then place the dough in a bowl, cover with a damp cloth and let stand for 10 minutes.

4 Line 1 large or 2 smaller steamers with the cabbage leaves. Add the dumplings and steam, covered, over boiling water for 20 minutes. Do not allow the pan to boil dry. Serve hot with a dipping sauce.

4½ cups flour	
1¼ cups water	
1 small cabbage, separated into leaves	
dipping sauce, to serve (see page 111)	
For the filling:	
1 pound boned chicken breasts, skinned	
8 ounces bamboo shoots, chopped	
3 scallions, finely chopped	
3 slices fresh gingerroot, peeled and finely chopped	
salt	
2 teaspoons sugar	
2 teaspoons light soy sauce	
2 tablespoons dry sherry	
2 tablespoons clear broth (see page 110)	
1 teaspoon sesame oil	

2 Meanwhile, make the filling for the dumplings. Cut the chicken into small bite-sized pieces and place in a bowl with the bamboo shoots, scallions, ginger, a little salt, the sugar, soy sauce, sherry, broth, and sesame oil. Mix well together.

3 Divide the dough in half and form each piece into a "sausage" shape. Cut each roll into 16 slices and then flatten into rounds. Roll out to circles, about 3 inches in diameter, and place 1 tablespoon of filling in the center of each one. Gather up the edges of the dough around the filling and twist at the top to seal.

PREPARATION: 45 MINUTES
COOKING: 20 MINUTES
SERVES: 8

SPRING ROLLS

Chun juan

1 Sift the flour and salt into a bowl and beat in the egg and 1¼ cups cold water until you have a smooth batter. Lightly oil an 8-inch skillet and set it over moderate heat. Pour in sufficient batter to cover the base.

2 Cook until the underside is pale golden and then turn the crepe over and cook the other side until golden. Repeat in the same way until all the batter is used.

3 Make the filling: heat the oil and then add the pork. Stir-fry for 2 to 3 minutes, until it is evenly browned. Add the garlic and vegetables and stir-fry for 2 minutes. Mix in the shrimp and soy sauce, then remove from the heat and allow to cool.

2 cups flour
pinch of salt
1 egg
1 tablespoon flour, mixed with 1 tablespoon water for the paste
corn oil for deep-frying
For the filling:
1 tablespoon corn oil
8 ounces lean pork, shredded
1 garlic clove, crushed
2 celery sticks, sliced
4 ounces mushrooms, sliced
2 scallions, chopped
4 ounces bean sprouts
1 cup peeled shrimp
2 tablespoons light soy sauce

PREPARATION: 35 MINUTES
COOKING: 10 MINUTES
SERVES: 4 TO 6

4 Place about 2 to 3 tablespoons of the filling in the center of each crepe. Fold in the sides and roll up tightly, sealing the edge with a little flour and water paste. Deep-fry the spring rolls in hot oil, two at a time, until evenly golden. Drain and serve hot.

STEAMED FISH

Qing zheng yu

1 Put the mushrooms in a bowl and cover with warm water. Leave to soak for 20 minutes. Squeeze the mushrooms dry and discard the stalks.

2 Slash both sides of the fish diagonally, as deep as the bone, at intervals of about ¹/₂ inch. This prevents the skin from bursting during cooking and allows the heat to penetrate more quickly. Dry the fish with paper towels and place it on a plate.

3 Thinly shred the fresh gingerroot, scallions, ham, bamboo shoots, and mushrooms. Arrange them on top of the fish.

2 Chinese dried mushrooms
1 (1-pound) striped bass, cleaned and scaled
2 slices fresh gingerroot, peeled
2 scallions
2 ounces cooked ham
2 ounces bamboo shoots
3 tablespoons dry sherry
2 tablespoons soy sauce
1 teaspoon sugar
1 teaspoon salt

PREPARATION: 10 MINUTES +
SOAKING TIME
COOKING: 15 MINUTES
SERVES: 2

4 Mix together the sherry, soy sauce, sugar, and salt, and pour over the fish. Place the fish on the plate in the top of a steamer set over simmering water. Cover and steam vigorously for 15 minutes. Serve hot.

SWEET & SOUR RED-COOKED FISH

Hongshao yu

1 Wash the fish and dry with paper towels. Using a sharp knife, slash both sides of the fish diagonally at ³/₄-inch intervals. Sprinkle with salt and dredge with flour.

1 (2-pound) whole fish, e.g. striped bass or porgy, cleaned and scaled
1 teaspoon salt
2 tablespoons flour
oil for deep-frying
3 tablespoons vegetable oil
½ ounce dried Chinese mushrooms, soaked for 20 minutes, drained and stemmed
2 ounces bamboo shoots, sliced
3 garlic cloves, crushed
4 scallions, shredded
3 slices fresh gingerroot, shredded
1 ounce water chestnuts, sliced
For the sweet and sour sauce:
1 tablespoon cornstarch
2 tablespoons light soy sauce
2 tablespoons sherry
1 tablespoon brown sugar
1 tablespoon vinegar
1 tablespoon tomato paste
4 tablespoons broth

2 Heat the oil for deep-frying in a wok or deep saucepan and when it is hot, add the fish. Fry for 6 to 8 minutes, until cooked and crisp. Turn the fish halfway through cooking to cook both sides. Remove and keep warm.

PREPARATION: 15 MINUTES
COOKING: 15 MINUTES
SERVES: 4

3 Heat the vegetable oil in a clean wok or skillet and add the mushrooms, bamboo shoots, garlic, scallions, ginger, and water chestnuts. Stir-fry briskly for 3 to 4 minutes.

4 Mix all the sauce ingredients together in a bowl and then stir into the vegetable mixture in the wok. Keep stirring over moderate heat until thickened. Arrange the fish on a serving dish and pour the sauce over the top. Serve immediately.

SQUID AND GREEN BELL PEPPERS

Si chiu chao yau

1 Clean the squid, discarding the head and transparent back bone as well as the ink bag. Wash the squid well under running cold water and then pat dry with paper towels.

8 ounces squid
1 green bell pepper, cored and seeded
2 slices fresh gingerroot, peeled
oil for deep-frying
1 teaspoon salt
1 tablespoon soy sauce
1 teaspoon vinegar
freshly ground black pepper
1 teaspoon sesame oil

3 Heat the oil in a wok or deep skillet until it is hot. Deep-fry the prepared squid for about 30 seconds and then remove. Carefully pour off the excess oil, leaving about 1 tablespoon of oil in the skillet. Add the ginger, bell pepper, and squid.

4 Stir-fry for a few seconds and then stir in the salt, soy sauce, vinegar, and black pepper. Cook for about 1 minute, and then add the sesame oil and serve.

2 Peel off the thin skin of the squid and cut the flesh into small pieces, about the size of a matchbox. Slice the green bell pepper and thinly shred the fresh gingerroot.

PREPARATION: 15 MINUTES
COOKING: 5 MINUTES
SERVES: 2 TO 4

GINGER AND SCALLION CRAB

Congjang xieh

1 Break off the legs of the crab and crack the shells into 2 or 3 pieces. Open the shell by laying the crab on its back and pressing down with your thumbs along the suture. Lift out and discard the stomach and intestine and the feathery gills. Crack the shell with a chopper or heavy knife.

1 (1½-pound) crab
2 tablespoons sherry
1 tablespoon clear broth (see page 110) or water
2 tablespoons cornstarch
4 slices fresh gingerroot, peeled
4 scallions
3 tablespoons oil
1 teaspoon salt
1 tablespoon soy sauce
2 teaspoons sugar

PREPARATION: 20 MINUTES
COOKING: 8 TO 10 MINUTES
SERVES: 2 TO 4

3 Finely chop the gingerroot and scallions. In a wok or deep skillet, heat the oil until it is very hot. Add the crabmeat to the wok and then fry briskly for about 1 minute, turning it in the oil.

2 Scrape out some of the meat from the shell and place in a bowl with the claws, etc. Mix 1 tablespoon of the sherry with the broth or water and cornstarch. Pour over the crab and leave to marinade for a few minutes.

4 Add the ginger, scallions, salt, soy sauce, sugar, and the remaining sherry. Cook for about 5 minutes, stirring all the time. Add a little water if the mixture becomes very dry. Serve immediately.

SEAFOOD WITH VEGETABLES

Zhuachao haixian

1 Cut each scallop into 3 or 4 pieces. Peel the shrimp and remove the black vein running along the back. Leave whole if small, or cut into 2 or 3 pieces if large. Put the seafood in a bowl with the egg white and half of the cornstarch, and mix well.

2 Heat the oil in a deep wok, and then deep-fry the scallops and shrimp for 1 minute, stirring all the time to keep the pieces separate. Remove the seafood and then drain on paper towels.

3 Pour off all but 2 tablespoons of oil from the wok. Increase the heat to high and add the vegetables, ginger, and scallions. Stir-fry for about 1 minute. Add the scallops and shrimp and stir in the sherry, soy sauce, chile bean paste (if using) and salt.

4-6 fresh scallops
1 cup headless uncooked shrimp
1 egg white
1 tablespoon cornstarch
vegetable oil for deep-frying
3 celery sticks, sliced
1 red bell pepper, seeded and sliced
1 to 2 carrots, sliced
2 slices fresh gingerroot, peeled and shredded
2 to 3 scallions, chopped
2 tablespoons sherry
1 tablespoon light soy sauce
2 teaspoons chile bean paste (optional)
1 teaspoon salt
1 teaspoon sesame oil, to finish

PREPARATION: 20 MINUTES
COOKING: 5 MINUTES
SERVES: 3 TO 4

4 Mix the remaining cornstarch to a smooth paste with a little water, and then add to the wok. Stir well until thickened. Sprinkle over the sesame oil and serve immediately.

SHRIMP WITH BROCCOLI

Jielan chao xiaqiu

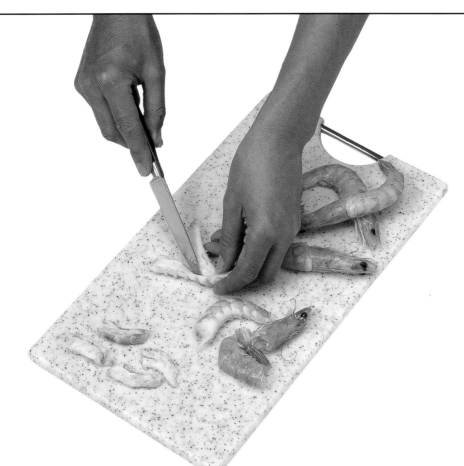

3 Heat 1 tablespoon of the oil in a wok or skillet and add the shrimp. Stir-fry over moderate heat for about 30 seconds and then remove from the wok or skillet.

1 Wash the shrimp, and dry thoroughly on paper towels. Shell the shrimp and remove the black intestinal veins. Split each shrimp in half lengthwise and then cut it into several small pieces.

8 ounces cooked jumbo shrimp in their shells
1 slice fresh gingerroot, peeled and finely chopped
1 tablespoon sherry
1 egg white
1 teaspoon cornstarch
3 tablespoons vegetable oil
2 scallions, finely chopped
8 ounces broccoli, cut into small pieces
1 teaspoon salt
1 teaspoon sugar

2 Put the shrimp pieces in a small bowl with the ginger, sherry, egg white, and cornstarch. Stir well and then leave in the refrigerator to marinate for about 20 minutes.

4 Heat the remaining oil in the wok or skillet. Add the scallions and broccoli and stir well. Add the salt and sugar and stir-fry until the broccoli is just tender. Add the shrimp and stir to mix with the broccoli. Serve hot.

PREPARATION: 10 MINUTES +
MARINATING TIME
COOKING: 5 MINUTES
SERVES: 2 TO 3

RAPID-FRIED SHRIMP

Tangcui daxia

1 | Wash and trim the shrimp, removing the legs but leaving the tail pieces firmly attached. Remove the black intestinal vein and pat dry with paper towels.

1 pound headless uncooked shrimp
vegetable oil for deep-frying
2 teaspoons cornstarch
For the sweet and sour sauce:
2 tablespoons dry sherry
2 tablespoons soy sauce
2 tablespoons vinegar
1 tablespoon sugar
1 teaspoon finely chopped scallion
1 teaspoon finely chopped fresh gingerroot

2 | Heat the oil in a deep wok or saucepan until it is very hot. Turn down the heat to allow the oil to cool a little, and then deep-fry the shrimp until they turn bright pink. Remove them from the wok or pan and then dry on paper towels.

3 | Pour off all but 1 tablespoon of oil from the wok, and increase the heat to high. Quickly mix together the sauce ingredients and add to the wok with the shrimp. Cook for about 1 minute, stirring.

4 | Mix the cornstarch to a smooth paste with 1 tablespoon cold water. Add to the wok and stir until all the shrimp are coated with the sauce.

PREPARATION: 10 MINUTES
COOKING: 5 MINUTES
SERVES: 4

STIR-FRIED SHRIMP

Xiaren chao xiangsu

1 Wash the shrimp, removing the heads, shells, and legs. Keep the tails intact. Dry thoroughly on paper towels and set aside.

4 Add the garlic, black beans, snow peas, and water chestnuts to the wok and stir-fry for 1-2 minutes. Return the shrimp to the wok. Mix the remaining cornstarch with the soy sauce and chicken broth and stir into the shrimp mixture until thickened. Add the sesame oil and toss well.

2 Heat the vegetable oil in a deep wok or large skillet until it starts to smoke. Add the slices of fresh gingerroot and fry for 30 seconds to flavor the oil, then remove and discard the ginger.

3 In a bowl, mix together 2 tablespoons of the cornstarch with the salt, sherry, and egg white. Toss the shrimp in this mixture until well coated. Add the shrimp to the hot oil and stir-fry until they change color. Remove and set aside.

1 pound uncooked jumbo shrimp
4 tablespoons vegetable oil
3 slices fresh gingerroot, peeled
2 tablespoons cornstarch, plus 1 teaspoon
1 teaspoon salt
1 tablespoon dry sherry
1 egg white
2 garlic cloves, crushed
2 teaspoons black beans, soaked for 1 hour and drained
8 ounces snow peas, trimmed and cut in half
6 water chestnuts, thinly sliced
1/2 tablespoon soy sauce
2 tablespoons chicken broth
1 teaspoon sesame oil

PREPARATION: 10 MINUTES
COOKING: 8 TO 10 MINUTES
SERVES: 3 TO 4

PAPER-WRAPPED FISH

Zhibao yu

1 Cut the fish fillets into 1-inch squares, about ¼-inch thick. Place them in a bowl and then sprinkle with the salt and sherry. Leave to marinate for 10 minutes.

3 Fold the pieces of paper into envelopes, tucking in the flaps to secure them well. Heat the oil to 350°F in a wok or deep saucepan.

2 Cut out a 6-inch square of waxed paper for each piece of fish. Brush with oil. Place a piece of fish on each piece of paper and top with some shredded scallions and gingerroot.

4 (4-ounce) fillets of orange roughy or flounder
pinch of salt
2 tablespoons dry sherry
1 tablespoon vegetable oil
2 tablespoons shredded scallions
2 tablespoons shredded fresh gingerroot
vegetable oil for deep-frying
To garnish:
scallion tassels (see page 110)

4 Deep-fry the wrapped fish for 3 minutes, until golden on both sides. Remove carefully and then drain the fish on paper towels. Arrange on a serving dish garnished with scallion tassels, if using. The paper wrappings are opened by the guests.

PREPARATION: 15 MINUTES +
MARINATING TIME
COOKING: 3 MINUTES
SERVES: 4

SWEET AND SOUR PORK

Kulu rou

1 Cut the pork into 24 small cubes. Cut the bamboo shoots and green bell pepper into small chunks. Cut the spring onions into 1-inch lengths.

3 Heat the oil in a wok or saucepan. Coat each piece of pork with the flour and deep-fry for 3 minutes. Remove the wok from the heat but leave the pork in the oil for a further 2 minutes before removing and draining. Return the wok to the heat and re-fry the meat with the bamboo shoots for 2 minutes. Remove and drain.

2 Place the pork in a bowl and sprinkle with the salt and brandy. Set aside to marinate for 15 minutes. Add the beaten egg and cornstarch and blend well.

PREPARATION: 15 MINUTES + MARINATING TIME
COOKING: 15 MINUTES
SERVES: 3 TO 4

8 ounces pork
4 ounces bamboo shoots
1 green bell pepper, cored and seeded
2 scallions
1 teaspoon salt
1 1/2 tablespoons brandy
1 egg, beaten
1 tablespoon cornstarch
oil for deep-frying
3 tablespoons flour
2 cups canned pineapple chunks in juice
For the sauce:
3 tablespoons vinegar
3 tablespoons sugar
1/2 teaspoon salt
1 tablespoon tomato paste
1 tablespoon soy sauce
1 tablespoon cornstarch
1 teaspoon sesame oil

4 Pour off the excess oil, leaving 1 tablespoonful in the wok. Add the scallons and green bell pepper. Mix the sauce ingredients with a little canned pineapple juice and add to the wok, stirring until thickened. Add the pork, bamboo shoots, and pineapple and serve hot.

BARBECUED PORK

Cha shao

1 Trim off any excess fat from the loin of pork and then cut the meat into 2 x 2 x 4-inch slices. Mix together all the ingredients for the marinade in a dish.

2 pounds boned loin of pork
For the marinade:
2 tablespoons soy sauce
2 tablespoons dry sherry
2 teaspoons sesame oil
1 teaspoon salt
2 teaspoons ginger juice (squeezed from chopped fresh gingerroot)
2 tablespoons clear honey
4 tablespoons sugar
2 garlic cloves, crushed
To garnish:
shredded scallions

PREPARATION: 10 MINUTES +
MARINATING TIME
COOKING: 40 TO 45 MINUTES
SERVES: 6

2 Add the pork to the marinade and leave to marinate for at least 6 hours in the refrigerator. Turn the meat occasionally so that it is well coated with marinade.

3 Place the pork on a wire rack in a roasting pan. Roast in a preheated oven at 350°F for 40 to 45 minutes, or until tender. Baste the pork frequently with the pan juices.

4 Cut the cooked pork into serving pieces and arrange them on a plate. Garnish with shredded scallions and serve immediately.

PORK IN BLACK BEAN SAUCE

Rousi chao ringjiao

1 Mix together the soy sauce, sherry, sugar, and flour in a large bowl. Add the ribs, and set aside in a cool place to marinate for 10 to 15 minutes.

2 Heat the oil in a wok or skillet and add the pork ribs. Stir-fry for a few minutes until they are golden. Remove the ribs and drain on paper towels.

3 Add the garlic, scallions, and bean sauce to the wok and stir well. Add the ribs with the broth or water, and cook, covered, over high heat for 5 minutes. If necessary, add a little more liquid, replace the lid and cook for a further 5 minutes.

1 tablespoon soy sauce
2 tablespoons dry sherry
1 tablespoon sugar
1 tablespoon plain flour
1 pound pork ribs, chopped into small pieces
3 tablespoons oil
1 garlic clove, crushed
2 scallions, sliced diagonally
2 tablespoons crushed black or yellow bean sauce
5 tablespoons clear broth (see page 110) or water
1 small green bell pepper, seeded and sliced
1 small red bell pepper, seeded and sliced

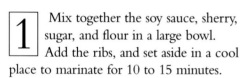

4 Add the sliced green and red bell peppers and stir well. Cook for 2 minutes and then remove from the heat. Serve immediately.

PREPARATION: 10 MINUTES +
MARINATING TIME
COOKING: 15 TO 20 MINUTES
SERVES: 4

RED-COOKED PORK

Hongshao zhuti

1 Put the mushrooms in a bowl and cover with warm water. Set aside to soak for 30 minutes. Squeeze the mushrooms dry and then discard the stems.

2 Put the pork in a large saucepan and cover with cold water. Bring to the boil, then boil for a few minutes and drain. Rinse the pork under running cold water and drain again.

PREPARATION: 15 MINUTES +
SOAKING TIME
COOKING: 2 TO 3 HOURS
SERVES: 4 TO 6

3 Wash the saucepan out and then return the pork to the clean pan. Add the mushrooms, garlic, soy sauce, sherry, sugar, and five-spice powder. Cover with a tight-fitting lid and bring to the boil.

4 Lower the heat and simmer very gently for 2 to 3 hours, turning the pork several times during cooking. There should be very little liquid left at the end of the cooking time. If necessary, increase the heat and simmer, uncovered, until reduced and thickened. Serve garnished with shredded scallions.

4 Chinese dried mushrooms
1 (3-pound) leg or shoulder of pork
1 garlic clove, crushed
6 tablespoons soy sauce
3 tablespoons dry sherry
3 tablespoons brown sugar
1 teaspoon five-spice powder
To garnish:
shredded scallions

RED-OIL DUMPLINGS
Hongyou shuijiao

1 Sift the flour into a large bowl. Pour on ⅝ cup boiling water and stir to form a firm dough. Leave for a few minutes and then add 5 tablespoons cold water. Knead well to form a smooth dough.

3 Form the dough into a long sausage, and divide into 2-inch lengths. Roll each piece into a ball and then roll flat into a small pancake. Place about 1 tablespoon of the filling on each pancake and fold over to form a half-circle. Pinch the edges firmly to seal.

2 In a bowl, mix together the pork, shrimp, gingerroot, scallions, salt, soy sauce, sugar, water, Chinese cabbage, pepper, and oil. Beat together to form a paste.

PREPARATION: 25 MINUTES
COOKING: 5 TO 6 MINUTES
SERVES: 6

4½ cups flour
1 pound ground pork
¾ cup cooked peeled shrimp, finely chopped
1 tablespoon chopped fresh gingerroot
1 tablespoon chopped scallions
1½ teaspoons salt
1 tablespoon soy sauce
1 teaspoon sugar
1 tablespoon water
2 leaves Chinese cabbage, finely chopped
pinch of ground pepper
2 teaspoons sesame oil
For the dipping sauce:
1 scallion, finely chopped
1 garlic clove, finely chopped
2 tablespoons peanut butter
2 teaspoons soy sauce
1 teaspoon red chile oil
2 teaspoons chicken broth

4 Cook the dumplings in boiling water for 5 to 6 minutes. Meanwhile, mix together the dipping sauce ingredients. Drain the hot dumplings and serve with the sauce.

PORK AND VEGETABLES

Chop suey

8 ounces pork loin
2 tablespoons soy sauce
1 tablespoon dry sherry
2 teaspoons cornstarch
2 scallions
1 slice fresh gingerroot, peeled
4 ounces fresh bean sprouts
5 tablespoons oil
1 small green bell pepper, cored and seeded
few cauliflower or broccoli florets
2 to 3 tomatoes, cut into pieces
2 carrots, cut into matchsticks
2 ounces thin green beans, trimmed
2 teaspoons salt
1 tablespoon sugar
3 tablespoons clear broth (see page 110) or water

2 Cut the scallions into 1-inch lengths and finely chop the fresh gingerroot. Wash the bean sprouts in a basin of cold water and discard any husks that float to the surface.

3 Heat half of the oil in a wok or heavy skillet. Stir-fry the sliced pork for about 1 minute and then remove it from the wok and put to one side while you stir-fry the vegetables.

1 Cut the pork loin into small, thin slices. Mix together the soy sauce, sherry, and cornstarch in a bowl, and add the pork. Stir well until each slice is coated with the mixture.

4 Heat the remaining oil and add the scallions and gingerroot, followed by the rest of the vegetables and the salt and sugar. Stir-fry for 1 to 2 minutes and then add the sliced pork. Moisten with a little broth or water if wished and stir-fry quickly until the vegetables are tender but still crisp. Serve immediately with rice.

PREPARATION: 15 MINUTES
COOKING: 8 TO 10 MINUTES
SERVES: 3 TO 4

GINGER BEEF WITH BELL PEPPERS

Gungchung si chiu ghao

1 Put the slices of fillet steak in a bowl and add the soy sauce, 1 teaspoon of the sesame oil, the sliced gingerroot, vinegar, water, salt, and cornstarch. Stir well to mix, until the steak slices are coated thoroughly. Cover and leave in the refrigerator to marinate for at least 20 minutes.

2 Heat the remaining sesame oil in a wok or skillet and add the garlic and five-spice powder. Stir-fry for 30 seconds and then add the marinaded steak slices. Stir-fry quickly until the meat is browned on the outside yet still pink and tender on the inside. Remove the steak and set aside.

3 Add the chunks of red and green bell pepper to the wok or skillet, and stir-fry briskly for 2 to 3 minutes, tossing them in the oil.

1 pound lean fillet steak, thinly sliced
2 teaspoons soy sauce
2 tablespoons sesame oil
1-inch piece fresh gingerroot, peeled and sliced
2 teaspoons vinegar
1 tablespoon water
1 teaspoon salt
1 teaspoon cornstarch
1 garlic clove, crushed
pinch of five-spice powder
1 red bell pepper, seeded and cut into chunks
1 green bell pepper, seeded and cut into chunks
To garnish:
slivers of fresh red chile

4 Add the strips of steak and any remaining marinade. Stir-fry for 1 minute, until the meat is heated through. Transfer to a serving dish and serve garnished with thin slivers of chile.

PREPARATION: 10 MINUTES
+ MARINATING TIME
COOKING: 5 MINUTES
SERVES: 3 TO 4

BEEF WITH CASHEWS

Yeu gua chao ghao

1 Cut the fillet steak into thin slices, removing any fat. Place in a bowl and add the soy sauce, sherry, 2 teaspoons of the sesame oil, the water, cornstarch, seasoning, and gingerroot. Cover and leave in the refrigerator to marinate for at least 20 minutes.

2 Heat the remaining sesame oil in a deep wok or heavy skillet. Remove the strips of steak from the marinade and stir-fry quickly in the hot oil for 2 minutes, until brown and sealed on the outside. Remove and set aside. Reserve the marinade.

3 Add the garlic, cashews, and celery to the wok or skillet, and then stir-fry quickly over moderate heat for 2 to 3 minutes, tossing well.

1 pound lean fillet steak
2 tablespoons soy sauce
1 tablespoon dry sherry
3 tablespoons sesame oil
3 tablespoons water
2 teaspoons cornstarch
salt and freshly ground black pepper
1 tablespoon finely chopped peeled fresh gingerroot
2 garlic cloves, crushed
1 cup unsalted roasted cashews
3 celery sticks, sliced diagonally

4 Return the steak to the wok with the reserved marinade and mix well with the nuts and celery. Increase the heat and continue cooking, stirring all the time, until the sauce thickens. Transfer to a serving dish.

PREPARATION: 10 MINUTES +
MARINATING TIME
COOKING: 8 MINUTES
SERVES: 3 TO 4

BEEF IN OYSTER SAUCE

Hao yiu niu jou

1 Cut the beef into thick slices, about the size of a matchbox. In a bowl, mix together the oyster sauce, sherry, and cornstarch, and marinate the beef in this mixture for about 20 minutes.

2 Cut the broccoli into small florets. Slice the bamboo shoots and carrot into slices, about the same size as the beef slices. If using Chinese dried mushrooms, soak them in warm water for 20 minutes, squeeze dry, discard the stalks, and finely slice the mushrooms.

8 ounces beef steak
2 tablespoons oyster sauce
1 tablespoon dry sherry
1 tablespoon cornstarch
4 ounces broccoli
4 ounces bamboo shoots
1 carrot, peeled
4 ounces button mushrooms or 3 to 4 Chinese dried mushrooms
4 tablespoons oil
2 slices fresh gingerroot, peeled and chopped
2 scallions, chopped
1 teaspoon salt
1 teaspoon sugar
2 tablespoons clear broth (see page 110) or water

PREPARATION: 15 MINUTES +
MARINATING TIME
COOKING: 5 MINUTES
SERVES: 4

3 Heat half of the oil in a wok or heavy skillet. Add the beef and stir-fry for 10 to 15 seconds. Remove the beef and set aside.

4 Heat the remaining oil and then add the gingerroot and scallions, followed by all the vegetables. Add the salt and sugar and stir-fry for 1½ minutes. Add the beef, stir well, and moisten with a little broth or water. Heat through and serve immediately.

ROAST PEKING DUCK

Beijing kao ya

1 Wash the duck and pat dry with paper towels. Dissolve the sugar and salt in the water and rub all over the duck. Leave for several hours in the refrigerator or a cool place until dry. Place the duck in a roasting pan and then cook in a preheated oven at 400°F for 1 hour.

2 Prepare the vegetables for serving with the duck. Make some scallion flowers by making several cuts from top to bottom along each scallion, without cutting through the base. Leave in a bowl of iced water to open. Cut the leeks and cucumber into 3-inch strips and then arrange on a dish with the scallions.

3 Just before the duck is ready, make the sauce. Put all the ingredients in a small saucepan and heat gently over low heat for 2 to 3 minutes, stirring constantly. Pour the sauce into a small serving bowl.

1 (3-4 pound) duckling
1 tablespoon sugar
1 teaspoon salt
1¼ cups water
For the sauce:
3 tablespoons yellow bean sauce
2 tablespoons sugar
1 tablespoon sesame oil
To serve:
12 scallions
4 leeks
½ cucumber
24 Mandarin Pancakes (see page 110)

PREPARATION: 25 MINUTES +
STANDING TIME
COOKING: 1 HOUR
SERVES: 4 TO 6

4 Put the roasted duck on a serving dish and tear the meat off the bones with a fork, or, alternatively, carve it into neat slices. Serve with the Mandarin Pancakes and sauce. Each person spreads a little sauce on each pancake, places a little leek and cucumber in the middle plus some duck, and then rolls the pancake up.

SHREDDED CHICKEN AND CELERY

Yuxiang jisi

1 Cut the chicken breast meat into shreds and place in a bowl. Add the salt, egg white, and cornstarch and mix well. Cut the celery, green bell pepper, gingerroot, and scallions into slivers, the same size as the chicken.

2 Heat the oil in a wok or heavy skillet and add the chicken shreds. Stir-fry over moderate heat until the chicken is lightly and evenly colored. Remove the chicken from the wok and set aside.

3 Increase the heat and, when the oil is very hot, add the gingerroot and scallions followed by the celery and green bell pepper. Stir-fry for about 30 seconds over high heat.

4 Return the chicken shreds to the wok with the soy sauce and sherry. Mix well and cook for a further 1 to 1¹/₂ minutes, stirring all the time. Transfer to a serving dish and serve immediately.

8 ounces chicken breast meat, boned and skinned
¹/₂ teaspoon salt
1 egg white
1 tablespoon cornstarch
1 small celery stick
1 green bell pepper, cored and seeded
4 slices fresh gingerroot, peeled
2 scallions
4 tablespoons oil
2 tablespoons soy sauce
1 tablespoon dry sherry

PREPARATION: 15 MINUTES
COOKING: 7 TO 8 MINUTES
SERVES: 3 TO 4

CHICKEN WITH WALNUTS

Kung bao jiding

1 Cut the chicken flesh into small cubes, about the size of sugar lumps. Place them in a bowl with the salt, and then mix in the egg white. Finally, mix in 1 tablespoon of the cornstarch.

2 Heat the oil in a wok or heavy skillet and, when it is really hot, add the cubes of chicken. Stir-fry them briskly for a few minutes until the color of the chicken changes from pink to white. Remove them from the wok and set aside.

3 Add the scallions, ginger, chiles, and walnuts to the hot oil in the wok, and then stir in the bean sauce. Stir a few times and then add the green bell pepper. Return the chicken to the wok and stir well. Add the sugar and sherry, and stir-fry for about 1 minute.

12 ounces boneless chicken breasts, skinned
½ teaspoon salt
1 egg white
1 tablespoon cornstarch, plus 1 teaspoon
4 tablespoons vegetable oil
2 scallions, cut into ½-inch lengths
2 slices fresh gingerroot, peeled
3 to 4 dried red chiles, thinly sliced
½ cup shelled walnuts, roughly chopped
1 tablespoon yellow or black bean sauce
1 green bell pepper, seeded and cut into chunks
1 teaspoon sugar
2 tablespoons dry sherry

4 Mix the remaining teaspoon of cornstarch to a smooth paste with 1 tablespoon of cold water. Add this mixture to the wok and blend well until thickened. Transfer to a warm serving dish and serve immediately.

PREPARATION: 15 MINUTES
COOKING: 5 MINUTES
SERVES: 3 TO 4

STIR-FRIED SESAME CHICKEN
Mala jiding

1 Toss the chicken cubes in the cornstarch until they are evenly coated. Heat the oil in a wok or skillet and, when really hot, add the chicken cubes. Stir-fry over high heat for 45 seconds and then remove from the wok. Set aside.

2 Add the green bell pepper to the hot oil in the wok, and stir-fry briskly over moderate heat for 1 minute. Stir in 1 tablespoon of the soy sauce and then remove the green bell pepper and set aside.

3 Add the lard to the wok and, when it has melted, add the remaining soy sauce, the sesame seed paste, sesame oil, broth or water, chile sauce, and sherry. Mix well together and cook for 1 minute.

1 pound boned chicken breasts, cut into 1-inch cubes
1½ teaspoons cornstarch
3½ tablespoons oil
1 green bell pepper, seeded and cut into 1-inch pieces
2½ tablespoons soy sauce
1 tablespoon lard
2½ tablespoons sesame seed paste
1 tablespoon sesame oil
1 tablespoon broth or water
1 teaspoon chile sauce
1 tablespoon dry sherry

To garnish:

sesame seeds

PREPARATION: 10 MINUTES
COOKING: 7 TO 8 MINUTES
SERVES: 3 TO 4

4 Return the chicken cubes to the sauce mixture in the wok, and stir over high heat for about 45 seconds. Mix in the reserved green bell pepper. Cook for a further 30 seconds until the pepper is just tender. Transfer to a serving dish and serve immediately, garnished with sesame seeds.

FRIED EIGHT-PIECE CHICKEN

Shao ba kuai

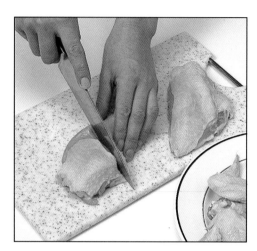

1 Wash the chicken inside and out, and then pat dry with paper towels. Carefully cut off the legs, wings, and breasts from the chicken, and then cut each breast in half.

3 Remove the chicken from the marinade and coat each piece with cornstarch. Reserve any leftover marinade. Meanwhile, heat the lard in a wok or large skillet.

2 In a large bowl, mix together the scallions and fresh gingerroot with 1 tablespoon of the sherry, 1 teaspoon of the sugar, and 1 tablespoon of the soy sauce. Add the chicken pieces and turn in the marinade until well coated. Leave in a cool place to marinade for about 5 minutes.

1 (2½-pound) chicken or Cornish hen
2 to 3 scallions, finely chopped
2 to 3 slices fresh gingerroot, finely chopped
2 tablespoons dry sherry
1 tablespoon sugar
3 tablespoons soy sauce
3 tablespoons cornstarch
1 stick lard
1 teaspoon sesame oil
To garnish:
chopped chives

PREPARATION: 20 MINUTES
COOKING: 15 MINUTES
SERVES: 4

4 Add the chicken to the wok and fry over moderate heat until golden brown all over and cooked through. Pour off the excess lard and add the remaining sherry, sugar, soy sauce, and leftover marinade. Bring to the boil, stirring. Stir in the sesame oil and then serve the chicken pieces immediately, garnished with chives.

NOODLES WITH CRAB SAUCE

Congjang mian

1 Fill a large saucepan with salted water and bring it to the boil. Throw in the egg noodles and boil rapidly for 5 minutes, or until they are just tender but still firm.

2 Drain the cooked noodles in a colander and when they are thoroughly dry, transfer them to a warmed serving dish. Set aside in a warm place while you prepare the sauce.

PREPARATION: 10 MINUTES
COOKING: 15 MINUTES
SERVES: 2 TO 3

3 Wash the spinach or cabbage leaves thoroughly and then drain and pat dry with paper towels. Cut into rough pieces. Heat the oil in a wok or heavy skillet and add the crabmeat and spinach or cabbage. Stir-fry for 1 minute.

4 Add the soy sauce and broth to the wok and cook briskly for 2 to 3 minutes, stirring occasionally. Pour the crabmeat sauce over the warm egg noodles and sprinkle with chopped scallion to garnish. Serve immediately.

pinch of salt	
5 ounces egg noodles	
4 ounces fresh spinach or cabbage	
2 tablespoons oil	
1/2 cup drained canned crabmeat	
1 teaspoon soy sauce	
1 cup clear broth (see page 110)	
To garnish:	
1 scallion, finely chopped	

NOODLES IN SOUP

Tang mian

1 Put the shrimp in a bowl with a pinch of salt. Mix the cornstarch to a smooth paste with 1 tablespoon cold water, and then stir into the shrimp. Thinly shred the bamboo shoots or mushrooms, and the spinach or bok choy.

2 Fill a large saucepan with salted water and bring to the boil. Add the egg noodles and boil until just tender. Drain well and place the noodles in a large warmed serving bowl or 4 individual bowls. Bring the broth to the boil and pour over the noodles with half of the soy sauce. Keep warm.

4 Stir a few times, and then add 1½ teaspoons salt, the remaining soy sauce, and the sherry. Cook for 1 to 2 minutes, stirring constantly. Pour the mixture over the noodles and sprinkle with sesame oil. Serve hot.

| 2 cups cooked peeled shrimp |
| salt |
| 1 teaspoon cornstarch |
| 4 ounces bamboo shoots or button mushrooms |
| 4 ounces spinach leaves or bok choy |
| 12 ounces egg noodles |
| 2½ cups chicken broth |
| 2 tablespoons light soy sauce |
| 3 tablespoons vegetable oil |
| 2 scallions, thinly shredded |
| 2 tablespoons dry sherry |
| 1 to 2 teaspoons sesame oil, to finish |

3 Heat the oil in a wok or skillet and add the shredded scallions to flavor the oil. Add the shrimp mixture and the shredded bamboo shoots or mushrooms and spinach or bok choy.

PREPARATION: 15 MINUTES
COOKING: 15 MINUTES
SERVES: 4

CHOW MEIN FRIED NOODLES
Chao mian

1 Fill a large saucepan with salted water and bring to the boil. Add the egg noodles and cook until tender but still firm. Drain in a colander and rinse under cold running water until cool. Set aside.

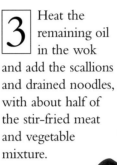 3 Heat the remaining oil in the wok and add the scallions and drained noodles, with about half of the stir-fried meat and vegetable mixture.

2 Heat about 3 tablespoons of the oil in a hot wok or skillet. Add the onion, shredded meat, snow peas, and bean sprouts, and stir-fry for 1 minute. Add 1 teaspoon of salt and stir a few more times. Remove from the wok and keep warm.

PREPARATION: 15 MINUTES
COOKING: 10 MINUTES
SERVES: 3 TO 4

1 pound egg noodles
salt
4 tablespoons vegetable oil
1 onion, thinly sliced
4 ounces cooked meat, e.g. pork, chicken, or ham, shredded
4 ounces snow peas, trimmed
4 ounces fresh bean sprouts
2 to 3 scallions, thinly shredded
2 tablespoons light soy sauce
1 tablespoon sesame oil or chile sauce, to finish

4 Mix in the soy sauce and stir-fry for 1 to 2 minutes, or until heated through. Transfer the mixture to a warmed serving dish and pour the remaining stir-fried meat and vegetable mixture over the top. Sprinkle with sesame oil or chile sauce and serve immediately.

SZECHUAN NOODLES

Dan dan mian

1 Bring a large saucepan of salted water to the boil. Add the thin egg noodles and cook, according to the packet instructions, until tender. Drain well and divide between 4 individual bowls or one large one.

2 Put the ground pork in a bowl with the soy sauce, sherry, and ½ teaspoon salt. Mix well to coat the pork thoroughly. Heat the oil in a deep wok or skillet, and add the pork. Stir-fry until lightly browned. Remove the pork from the wok and then dry on paper towels.

3 Add the garlic, ginger, scallions, and chiles to the wok and stir-fry for 1 minute. Add the hot soy bean paste and peanut butter, and stir well over moderate heat for a few seconds.

4 Add the chicken broth, bring to the boil and then simmer for about 5 minutes, until thickened. Stir in the pork and continue cooking over low heat for 1 minute. Spoon the sauce over the noodles and sprinkle with plenty of pepper. Garnish with chile.

salt
12 ounces thin egg noodles
1 cup ground pork
2 tablespoons dark soy sauce
1 tablespoon dry sherry
4 tablespoons peanut or vegetable oil
3 garlic cloves, crushed
1-inch piece fresh gingerroot, peeled and finely chopped
3 scallions, chopped
1 to 2 fresh red chiles, seeded and finely chopped
1 tablespoon hot soy bean paste
1 tablespoon peanut butter
¾ cup chicken broth
freshly ground black pepper
To garnish:
chopped fresh red chile

PREPARATION: 15 MINUTES
COOKING: 10 MINUTES
SERVES: 4

83

NOODLES WITH SHRIMP SAUCE

Lo mein

salt
1 pound egg noodles
3 ounces dried Chinese mushrooms
2 tablespoons vegetable oil
6 ounces boned, skinned chicken, diced
1 garlic clove, crushed
2 slices fresh gingerroot, peeled and chopped
4 scallions, cut diagonally into 1/2-inch pieces
1 1/2 cups shelled shrimp
2 tablespoons soy sauce
2 tablespoons dry sherry
3 3/4 cups clear broth (see page 110)
2 tablespoons cornstarch
2 ounces cooked lean ham, shredded

3 Heat the oil in a deep wok or large saucepan. Add the chicken, garlic, and ginger, and stir-fry for 2 to 3 minutes. Add the scallions and Chinese mushrooms and stir-fry for 2 minutes.

1 Bring a large saucepan of salted water to the boil and add the egg noodles. Boil rapidly according to packet instructions until they are just tender. Drain and divide the noodles between 6 serving dishes. Keep warm.

PREPARATION: 10 MINUTES + SOAKING TIME
COOKING: 20 MINUTES
SERVES: 6

2 While the noodles are cooking, place the dried Chinese mushrooms in a bowl, cover with warm water and leave to soak for 20 minutes. Drain, reserving the soaking liquid. Discard the stems and slice the caps thinly.

4 Add the shrimp, soy sauce, sherry, 1/2 teaspoon salt, and the clear broth. Bring to the boil and then simmer over gentle heat for 5 minutes. Mix the cornstarch with a little water and stir into the liquid in the wok. Keep stirring over low heat until it thickens slightly. Pour over the noodles, sprinkle with the shredded ham and serve

STEAMED MEAT DUMPLINGS

Shao bao

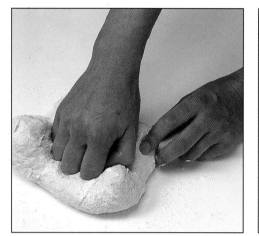

1 Sift the flour and baking powder into a mixing bowl. Mix in the water and knead well to make a smooth dough. Cover the bowl with a damp cloth and place a small plate on top. Leave the dough to rise at room temperature for 2 hours.

2 Meanwhile, make the filling: put the ground pork in a bowl with the sherry, soy sauce, sugar, salt, sesame oil, gingerroot, and cornstarch. Mix well together to coat the meat thoroughly.

3 Divide the dough in half, place on a lightly floured surface, and knead well. Shape each half into a long sausage-like roll, 2 inches in diameter. Slice each roll into about 15 rounds. Flatten each round with the palm of your hand and then with a rolling pin. Roll out into pancakes, about 3 inches in diameter.

4¹/₂ cups flour
4 teaspoons baking powder
1 cup water
Spicy Dipping Sauce, to serve (see page 111)
For the filling:
2 cups ground pork (not too lean)
1 tablespoon sherry
3 tablespoons soy sauce
2 teaspoons sugar
1 teaspoon salt
1 tablespoon sesame oil
2 teaspoons finely chopped peeled fresh gingerroot
1 teaspoon cornstarch

PREPARATION: 30 MINUTES +
RISING TIME
COOKING: 20 MINUTES
SERVES: 6

4 Place a little of the filling in the center of each pancake, and gather the sides of the dough up around the filling to meet at the top. Twist the top to close tightly. Arrange the dumplings in a cheesecloth-lined steamer, cover and steam vigorously for 20 minutes. Serve hot with the Spicy Dipping Sauce.

SPECIAL EGG-FRIED RICE
Chao fan

1 Break the eggs into a small bowl and add 1 teaspoon of the finely chopped scallions and a pinch of the salt. Beat lightly together with a fork to combine them.

2 Heat about 1 tablespoon of the oil in a hot wok or heavy skillet and add the beaten egg mixture. Stir constantly until the eggs are scrambled and set. Remove the scrambled eggs from the wok and set aside in a bowl.

3 Heat the remaining oil in the wok, and add the shrimp, meat, bamboo shoots, peas, and the remaining chopped scallions. Stir-fry briskly for 1 minute, and then stir in the soy sauce.

| 2 to 3 eggs |
| 2 scallions, finely chopped |
| 2 teaspoons salt |
| 3 tablespoons vegetable oil |
| $^3/_4$ cup cooked peeled shrimp |
| 4 ounces cooked meat, e.g. chicken or pork, diced |
| 2 ounces bamboo shoots, diced |
| 4 tablespoons fresh or frozen peas, cooked |
| 1 tablespoon light soy sauce |
| 4 cups cold cooked rice |

To garnish:

chopped scallions

4 Stir-fry for 2 to 3 minutes and then add the cooked rice, together with the scrambled eggs and the remaining salt. Stir well to break up the scrambled eggs into small pieces and separate the grains of rice. Serve hot, garnished with chopped scallions.

PREPARATION: 10 MINUTES
COOKING: 8 TO 10 MINUTES
SERVES: 4

EGGPLANTS IN FRAGRANT SAUCE

Qiezi Szechuan

1 Remove the peel from the eggplants, and cut the flesh into strips about the size of French fries. Cut the pork into thin shreds, the size of matchsticks. Chop the scallions, gingerroot, and garlic.

2 Heat the oil for deep-frying in a deep wok or saucepan. When it is hot, add the eggplant and deep-fry for 1 to 2 minutes, until crisp and golden. Remove from the wok and drain on paper towels.

PREPARATION: 15 MINUTES
COOKING: 5 TO 7 MINUTES
SERVES: 2 TO 3

3 Carefully pour off the oil to leave only 1 tablespoonful in the wok or pan. Quickly stir-fry the scallions, ginger, and garlic, followed by the pork. Blend in the soy sauce, sherry, and chile sauce, and then add the eggplant. Stir-fry for 1 to 2 minutes.

8 ounces eggplants
4 ounces pork loin
2 scallions
1 slice fresh gingerroot, peeled
1 garlic clove, peeled
oil for deep-frying
1 tablespoon soy sauce
1 tablespoon dry sherry
2 teaspoons chile sauce
2 tablespoons cornstarch

4 Mix the cornstarch with a little water in a small bowl and then stir it into the eggplant mixture. When the sauce thickens, remove from the heat and serve immediately.

STIR-FRIED VEGETABLES

Zhi wu si bao

1 Cover the dried mushrooms with warm water, cover and leave to soak for 30 minutes. Drain them and squeeze dry. Discard the hard stems and slice the mushrooms thinly. If using fresh mushrooms, just wash and slice them.

2 Cut the bok choy or cabbage and carrots diagonally into thin slices. If the French beans are small, leave them whole. However, if they are long, cut them in half.

PREPARATION: 10 MINUTES +
SOAKING TIME
COOKING: 3 TO 4 MINUTES
SERVES: 3 TO 4

3 Heat the oil in a hot wok or heavy skillet until it is smoking. Reduce the heat and add the bok choy or cabbage and carrots. Stir-fry them briskly for 30 seconds.

5 to 6 Chinese dried mushrooms or 2 ounces button mushrooms
8 ounces bok choy or cabbage
6 ounces carrots, peeled
4 ounces French beans, trimmed
4 tablespoons vegetable oil
1 teaspoon salt
1 teaspoon sugar
1 tablespoon light soy sauce

4 Add the beans and mushrooms and continue stir-frying for 30 seconds. Add the salt and sugar and toss and turn the vegetables until well blended. Stir in the soy sauce and cook for 1 more minute. Transfer to a warmed serving dish and serve immediately.

93

CHINESE BRAISED VEGETABLES

Su shijin

5 to 6 Chinese dried mushrooms
8 ounces firm bean curd
salt
4 tablespoons vegetable oil
4 ounces carrots, sliced
4 ounces snow peas, trimmed
4 ounces bok choy or cabbage, shredded
2 scallions, cut into ½-inch lengths
4 ounces bamboo shoots, sliced
1 teaspoon sugar
1 tablespoon light soy sauce
1 teaspoon cornstarch
1 teaspoon sesame oil

3 Heat about half of the oil in a heavy-based saucepan. Add the bean curd pieces and fry until lightly browned on both sides. Remove the bean curd, and then heat the remaining oil in the pan. Add the vegetables and stir-fry for 2 minutes. Stir in the bean curd with 1 teaspoon salt, the sugar and soy sauce. Cover, reduce the heat and braise for 3 minutes.

1 Put the Chinese dried mushrooms in a bowl and cover with warm water. Set aside to soak for 30 minutes, and then drain well. Discard the hard stems, and cut the mushroom caps into thin slices.

2 Cut each cake of bean curd into 12 small pieces. Bring a saucepan of lightly salted water to the boil and add the bean curd. Boil for 2 to 3 minutes until firm. Remove the bean curd pieces and then drain well on paper towels.

4 Meanwhile, mix the cornstarch to a smooth paste with 1 tablespoon cold water. Stir into the braised vegetables in the pan. Increase the heat and continue stirring until the sauce thickens. Sprinkle in the sesame oil and serve immediately.

PREPARATION: 20 MINUTES + SOAKING TIME
COOKING: 15 MINUTES
SERVES: 4

STIR-FRIED GREEN BEANS

Chao doujiao

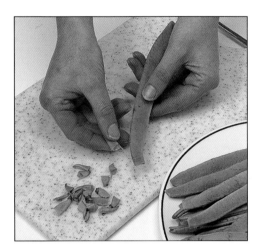

1 Top and tail the green beans and then remove the "strings" along the sides. Break the beans into 2-inch lengths. It does not matter if they are thin or thick beans.

3 Add the green beans and cashews to the wok and toss well to combine with the other vegetables and spices. Stir-fry quickly for 1 minute to brown the cashews.

1 pound green beans
3 tablespoons oil
2 garlic cloves, crushed
2 small onions, thinly sliced
1 slice fresh gingerroot, peeled and chopped
1 fresh red chile, seeded and finely chopped
1/2 teaspoon salt
1/2 cup unsalted cashews
1/2 cup chicken broth
2 tablespoons sherry
1 tablespoon light soy sauce
1 teaspoon vinegar
1 teaspoon sugar
freshly ground black pepper

2 Heat the oil in a deep wok or large skillet. Add the garlic, onions, and fresh gingerroot. Stir-fry briskly over moderate heat for 1 minute. Stir in the chile and salt and continue stir-frying for 30 seconds.

PREPARATION: 10 MINUTES
COOKING: 7 TO 8 MINUTES
SERVES: 4

4 Add the chicken broth, sherry, soy sauce, vinegar, and sugar to the wok and bring to the boil. Reduce the heat slightly and continue stir-frying for about 4 minutes, until the beans are cooked and the liquid has thickened. Serve immediately sprinkled with plenty of ground black pepper.

STIR-FRIED MUSHROOMS
Donggu ch'ao

3 Add the dried mushrooms and button mushrooms to the wok or pan and cook for 5 minutes, stirring all the time.

1 Put the dried shiitake mushrooms in a bowl and cover with boiling water. Leave them to soak for 15 minutes. Drain well and discard the hard stems.

2 ounces dried shiitake mushrooms, sliced
1 tablespoon oil
1 teaspoon finely chopped fresh gingerroot
2 scallions, finely chopped
1 garlic clove, crushed
8 ounces button mushrooms
1 (8-ounce) can straw mushrooms, drained
1 teaspoon chile bean sauce or chilli powder
2 teaspoons dry sherry
2 teaspoons dark soy sauce
1 tablespoon chicken broth
pinch of sugar
pinch of salt
1 teaspoon sesame oil

2 Heat the oil in a wok or deep skillet over moderate heat. Add the fresh gingerroot, scallions, and garlic and then stir-fry briskly for 5 to 10 seconds.

4 Add the straw mushrooms, chile bean sauce or chilli powder, sherry, soy sauce, chicken broth, sugar, salt, and sesame oil. Mix well and then stir-fry for 5 more minutes. Transfer to a warmed serving dish and serve.

PREPARATION: 5 MINUTES +
SOAKING TIME
COOKING: 10 MINUTES
SERVES: 4

SPICY VEGETABLES

Chao chop choi

1 Put the water in a large saucepan and bring to the boil. Add the cellophane noodles to the pan, bring back to the boil and boil rapidly for 3 minutes. Drain the noodles well and set aside.

2 Put the dried shiitake mushrooms in a bowl and cover with boiling water. Leave them to soak for about 20 minutes and then drain the mushrooms. Discard the hard stems and reserve the caps.

3 Heat 2 tablespoons of the oil in a deep wok or skillet, and add the cabbage and salt. Stir-fry for 2 minutes, and then remove. Heat the remaining oil in the wok or pan and stir-fry the carrot for 1 minute. Add the cabbage with the spinach and mushrooms and stir-fry for 2 minutes.

5 cups water
7 ounces transparent cellophane noodles
8 dried shiitake mushrooms
3 tablespoons corn oil
8 ounces Chinese cabbage or bok choy, shredded
pinch of salt
1 large carrot, thinly sliced
4 ounces fresh spinach, cooked and chopped
For the sauce:
1 tablespoon sesame oil
1 tablespoon soy sauce
2 teaspoons sugar
2 teaspoons sesame seeds
¹/₂ teaspoon salt

PREPARATION: 10 MINUTES + SOAKING TIME
COOKING: 15 MINUTES
SERVES: 4

4 Make the sauce: put all the ingredients in a pan over moderate heat and stir well. Bring to the boil and then pour over the vegetables in the wok. Add the cellophane noodles and toss well until thoroughly combined. Heat through and serve immediately.

LYCHEE SHERBET

Lichi bian choz ling

1 (1-pound) can of lychees
$^1/_2$ cup sugar
2 tablespoons lemon or lime juice
2 egg whites
To decorate:
thinly pared rind of 1 lime

1 Drain the juice from the lychees into a measuring jug and make up to 1$^1/_4$ cups with cold water. Pour into a saucepan and stir in the sugar. Heat gently, stirring, until the sugar has dissolved. Bring to the boil, then simmer gently for 10 minutes. Remove from the heat and let cool slightly.

2 Purée the lychees in a blender or food processor or press through a sieve. Mix with the sugar syrup and lemon or lime juice. Pour the mixture into a shallow freezer container and freeze for 1 to 2 hours, until nearly frozen.

3 Beat the egg whites in a clean, dry bowl until fairly stiff. Cut the frozen lychee mixture into small pieces and then work in a blender or food processor to break down the crystals. Transfer to a bowl and quickly fold in the beaten egg white. Pour into a freezer container and freeze for 2 to 3 hours, until firm.

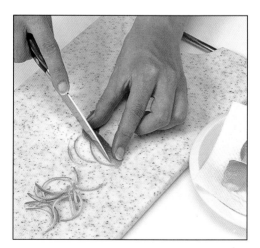

4 Plunge the pared lime rind into a saucepan of boiling water and blanch for 2 minutes. Drain, refresh, and pat dry. Cut into thin strips and serve sprinkled over the sherbet.

PREPARATION: 25 MINUTES
COOKING TIME: 10 MINUTES
FREEZING: 3 TO 5 HOURS
SERVES: 6

FRUIT FRITTERS

Basi shuiguo

1 Peel and core the apples and then cut each one into 8 pieces. Peel the bananas and cut each one in half lengthwise. Cut each half into 3 to 4 sections.

2 Make a batter: beat the egg in a small bowl and then blend in the cornstarch and sufficient cold water to make a smooth batter. Dip each piece of fruit into the batter.

3 Heat the oil for deep-frying in a deep wok or heavy saucepan, and when it is hot add the pieces of fruit in batter, a few at a time. Deep-fry for 2 to 3 minutes, until crisp and golden. Remove the fritters carefully and drain on paper towels.

2 large, firm apples
2 bananas
1 egg
4 tablespoons cornstarch
vegetable oil for deep-frying
1/2 cup sugar
3 tablespoons sesame oil
1 tablespoon sesame seeds
To serve:
fresh lime slices
banana slices

4 Heat the sugar and sesame oil over low heat for 5 minutes. Add 3 tablespoons of water and stir for 2 minutes. Add the fruit fritters and sesame seeds and stir slowly, until each fritter is coated with syrup. As soon as the syrup caramelizes, remove the fritters and plunge into a bowl of cold water to harden the "toffee." Serve with sliced lime and banana.

PREPARATION: 10 MINUTES
COOKING: 15 TO 20 MINUTES
SERVES: 6 TO 8

105

EIGHT-JEWEL RICE DESSERT
Babao fan

1 cup pearl rice
3 tablespoons lard
2 tablespoons sugar
30 raisins
10 walnut halves, chopped
1 (8-ounce) can of sweetened chestnut purée
4 candied cherries, sliced in half
4 pieces candied angelica
12 dried red dates, stoned
For the syrup:
3 tablespoons sugar
1¼ cups cold water
1 tablespoon cornstarch

1 Put the rice in a saucepan, cover with water and bring to the boil. Reduce the heat, cover tightly, and cook for 10 to 15 minutes, or until the water is absorbed. Add 2 tablespoons of the lard and the sugar to the rice. Mix well until the rice is thoroughly coated.

2 Brush a 1½-pint mold or bowl with the remaining lard. Cover the bottom and sides with a layer of the rice mixture. Mix together the raisins and nuts, and then arrange over the rice.

3 Cover with a thick layer of rice and fill the center with the chestnut purée. Cover with the remaining rice and flatten the top. Unmold carefully on to a plate and decorate the top with the cherries, angelica, and dates. Replace the mold over the dessert, turn over and remove the plate. Cover with a pleated circle of waxed paper secured with kitchen string.

4 Steam the dessert over a pan of simmering water for 1 hour. Dissolve the sugar for the syrup in the water and bring to the boil. Blend the cornstarch with 2 tablespoons of water. Add to the pan and simmer gently, stirring until thickened. Invert the rice dessert on to a plate, pour over the syrup, and serve immediately.

PREPARATION: 25 MINUTES
COOKING: 1 HOUR
SERVES: 6 TO 8

PEKING TOFFEE APPLES

Pa ssu ping kou

1 cup flour
1 egg
³/₈ cup water, plus 2 tablespoons
4 crisp apples, peeled, cored, and thickly sliced
corn oil for deep-frying, plus 1 tablespoon
6 tablespoons sugar
3 tablespoons light corn syrup

4 Add the fried apples to the syrup and make sure they are coated all over. Remove them and drop quickly into a bowl of iced water. Remove them immediately and serve.

1 In a bowl, mix together the flour, egg, and ³/₈ cup of the water, blending thoroughly to make a smooth batter. Dip each piece of apple into the batter.

3 Put the sugar and the remaining water and oil in a clean pan. Dissolve the sugar over gentle heat, stirring constantly. Add the light corn syrup and boil to the hard crack stage (304°F on a sugar thermometer). The syrup should form brittle threads when dropped into iced water.

2 In a wok or deep frying pan, heat the oil for deep-frying to 350°F, or until a cube of bread turns brown in 30 seconds. Add the battered apple pieces to the hot oil and deep-fry for 2 minutes until golden and crisp. Remove the apple fritters and drain on paper towels.

PREPARATION:
15 MINUTES
COOKING: 20 MINUTES
SERVES: 4

GARNISHES, RICE AND SAUCES

PLAIN RICE

1½ cups long-grain rice
3 cups water

Wash and rinse the rice in cold water, and then drain. Fill a saucepan with the water and bring to the boil over high heat. Add the washed rice and bring back to the boil. Cover the pan tightly with a lid and reduce the heat to a simmer. Cook gently for 20 minutes. Turn off the heat and leave the rice in the covered pan for another 10 minutes to dry out and avoid stickiness. Fluff the rice up with a fork before serving.
Serves 4 to 6

CLEAR BROTH
Qing tang

2 pounds chicken pieces
1½ pounds pork ribs
2 ounces fresh gingerroot, unpeeled and cut into chunks
4 to 5 scallions
12½ cups water
4 tablespoons Chinese rice wine or dry sherry

Trim off the excess fat from the chicken and pork, and then place in a large saucepan with the gingerroot and scallions. Pour in the water and bring to the boil.

Skim off any scum on the surface and then reduce the heat slightly. Cook, uncovered, for at least 1½ to 2 hours. Let cool. When cold, skim off any surface fat with a spoon.

Strain the broth and return to a clean saucepan. Add the rice wine or sherry and bring back to the boil.

Simmer for 5 minutes before using. The broth can be stored in a covered container in the refrigerator for 4 days. Makes 8½ cups

Note: This broth can be used as the base for a clear soup. Just add 2 teaspoons finely chopped onions, 1 tablespoon light soy sauce, and 1 teaspoon salt for every 2½ cups of stock.

SCALLION TASSELS

scallions

To make these tassels, trim the white ends and green leaves of the scallions so that they are 3 inches long. Cut along each one lengthwise through the stalk several times to within 1½ inches of the end. Place the scallions in a bowl of iced water for 1 hour until they open up like flowers. Use as an attractive garnish for many savory Chinese dishes.

MANDARIN PANCAKES
Bo bing

4½ cups flour
1¼ cups boiling water
a little vegetable oil

Sift the flour into a mixing bowl. Mix the boiling water with 1 teaspoon of oil, and then slowly stir into the flour with a wooden spoon. Knead the mixture on a lightly floured board until you have a firm dough, and then divide into 3 equal portions. Roll each portion into a long "sausage," and then cut each sausage into 8 equal pieces.

Press each piece into a flat pancake with the palm of your hand. Brush one pancake with a little oil, and then place another on top to form a "sandwich." Repeat with the remaining dough to make 12 sandwiches.

Flatten each sandwich into a 6-inch circle with a rolling pin on a lightly floured surface. Place an ungreased skillet over moderate heat and, when it is very hot, cook the sandwiches, one at a time. Turn them over as soon as air bubbles appear on the surface. Cook the other side until little brown spots appear underneath.

Remove from the pan and peel the 2 layers of each pancake apart. Serve the pancakes warm with Roast Peking Duck (see page 66).
Makes 24 pancakes

QUICK SWEET AND SOUR SAUCE

2 garlic cloves, crushed
1 tablespoon oil
2 tablespoons light soy sauce
2 tablespoons liquid honey
2 tablespoons wine vinegar
2 tablespoons tomato paste
2 teaspoons chile sauce
2 teaspoons Chinese wine or sherry
2 teaspoons cornstarch

Stir-fry the garlic in the oil for 2 minutes and then stir in all the remaining ingredients except the cornstarch. Mix the cornstarch with a little cold water to a smooth paste and then stir into the sauce. Bring to the boil, stirring all the time until the sauce thickens, and then cook for 2 minutes.
Serves 4

Spicy Dipping Sauce

2 tablespoons peanut butter
2 teaspoons soy sauce
1 teaspoon red chile oil
2 teaspoons chicken broth
1 garlic clove, crushed

Mix all the ingredients together and blend well to make a spicy dipping sauce for won tons, dumplings, and spring rolls. This sauce will serve 4 people.

Chinese Garnishes

The Chinese have always used attractive garnishes of vegetables and fruit to enhance the texture, color, flavor, and appearance of their dishes, particularly on formal occasions. Here are some ideas that you can try out yourself at home.

Radish Roses

You will need several fresh, unblemished radishes. Cut off the root end and trim the top of each radish. With a sharp knife, cut thin petals around the sides, starting at the stem end and finishing at the root.

Plunge the radishes into iced water and leave for 1 hour. Drain and pat dry before using as a garnish.

Tomato Lilies

You will need 2 or 3 firm, red tomatoes which are not too large. Insert a sharp knife into the side of the tomato at an angle and then work around the tomato, making "V" cuts as you go. Carefully separate the 2 halves, and you will have 2 attractive lily shapes. Repeat with the other tomatoes.

Tomato Roses

Alternatively, you can make tomato roses as a garnish. Using a sharp knife, peel off the skin, like an apple, in one piece, working from the top to the bottom of the tomato. Curl the skin into a circle and then invert it.

Cucumber Cartwheels

Take a small cucumber and using a sharp knife or potato peeler, cut small strips vertically from the peel from one end of the cucumber to the other at $1/2$-inch intervals. Remove the cut peel and discard. Slice the cucumber thinly.

Cucumber Twists

Alternatively, slice the cucumber thinly, leaving on the skin. Make one cut in each slice towards the center, but not all the way through. Twist both edges of the cucumber in opposite directions. You can make lemon twists in the same way.

Lemon Butterflies

Take a firm, evenly colored lemon and cut into thin slices horizontally. Cut out a quarter of the slice on each side to make a butterfly shape, leaving the center intact. Use to decorate sweet or savory dishes.

INDEX